Christmas Crafts

BY JEAN EICK • ILLUSTRATED BY KATHLEEN PETELINSEK

The Child's World

Published by The Child's World®
1980 Lookout Drive
Mankato, MN 56003-1705
800-599-READ
www.childsworld.com

The Child's World®: Mary Berendes, Publishing Director
The Design Lab: Design and production

Library of Congress Cataloging-in-Publication Data
Eick, Jean, 1947–
   Christmas crafts / by Jean Eick; illustrated by Kathleen Petelinsek.
      p. cm.
   ISBN 978-1-60954-232-0 (library bound: alk. paper)
   1. Christmas decorations—Juvenile literature. 2. Handicraft—Juvenile
literature. I. Petelinsek, Kathleen, ill. II. Title.
   TT900.C4E442 2011
   745.594'12—dc22   2010035497

Printed in the United States of America
Mankato, MN
December, 2010
PA02071

Table of Contents

It's Christmas Time!

Christmas is a special **holiday** for many people around the world. It is often celebrated on December 25. On this day, **Christians** celebrate the birthday of Jesus Christ.

People have celebrated Christmas for over a thousand years. In many **cultures**, it's a time to be with family and friends. Many people put up Christmas trees and listen to holiday music. Others bake special cookies, breads, and candies. Often, people give each other gifts at Christmas, too. Wherever you are in the world, Christmas is a time for sharing and kindness.

Let's Begin!

1 This book is full of great ideas you can make to celebrate Christmas. There are ideas for decorations, gifts, and cards. There are activities at the end of this book, too!

2 Before you start making any craft, be sure to read the **directions**. Make sure you look at the pictures, too—they will help you understand what to do. Go through the list of things you'll need and get everything together. When you're ready, find a good place to work. Now you can begin making your crafts!

Candy Canes

These decorations are easy to make. You can hang them on your Christmas tree or use them to decorate presents.

THINGS YOU'LL NEED

One red
pipe cleaner

One white
pipe cleaner

DIRECTIONS

1 Put the pipe cleaners side by side. Starting at one end, twist them together.

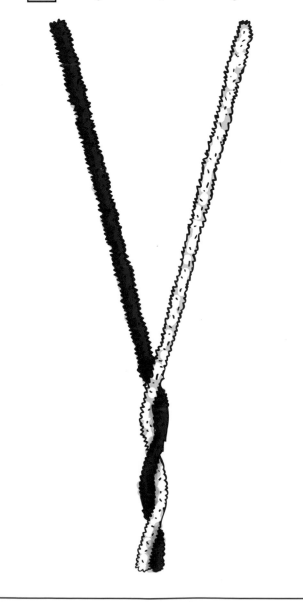

2 Do not twist too tightly—just firm enough to create a nice and even spiral shape.

3 Bend the top of the twisted pipe cleaners. Presto, a candy cane!

Rudolph

Everyone knows the story of Rudolph's red nose.
Now you can make a fun Rudolph decoration!

THINGS YOU'LL NEED

Scissors

2 sheets of brown construction paper

Pencil

Glue

Crayons or markers

Shoe

GLUE

BLUE

DIRECTIONS

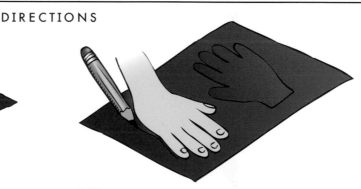

1 On one sheet of construction paper, draw around your shoe. This will be Rudolph's head.

2 On the other sheet, draw around each of your hands. These will be Rudolph's **antlers**.

3 Cut out the shoe and hand shapes.

4 Glue the handprints to the toe area of your shoe cutout.

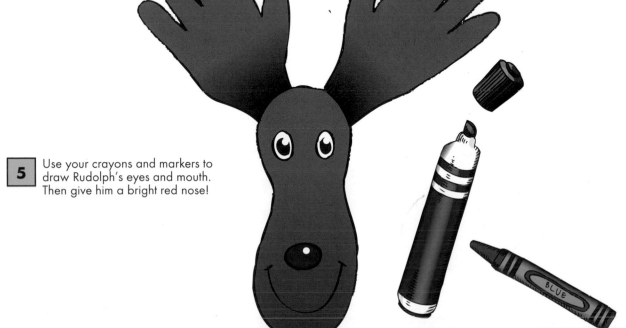

5 Use your crayons and markers to draw Rudolph's eyes and mouth. Then give him a bright red nose!

Christmas Strings

You can hang these easy decorations almost anywhere—even on your tree!

THINGS YOU'LL NEED

Scissors

3 sheets of construction paper:
1 red
1 white
1 green

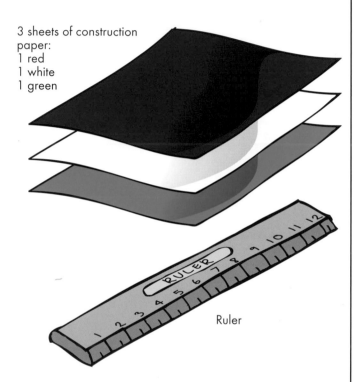

Tape

Pencil

Ruler

DIRECTIONS

1 With your ruler and pencil, **divide** each sheet of construction paper into strips. Each strip should be 1 inch wide by 6 inches long.

2 Cut the strips apart with your scissors.

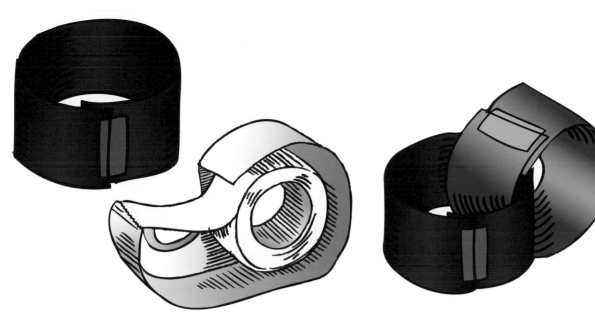

3 Tape the ends of one strip together to make a loop.

4 Take another strip (must be a different color than the first strip), and slip it through the first strip's paper ring. Then tape the ends together.

5 Do the same with another strip, and then another. Keep changing colors until you finish your chain.

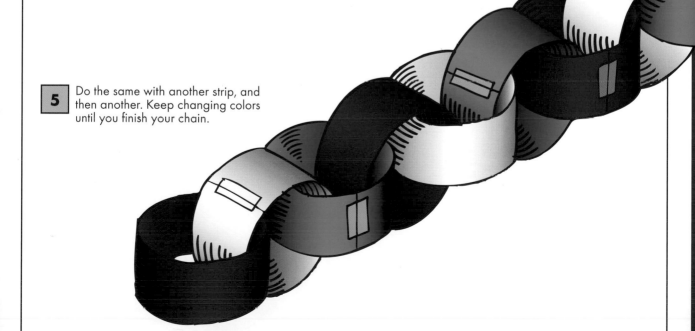

Bookmarks

Try making these pretty gifts for your friends and teachers.

THINGS YOU'LL NEED

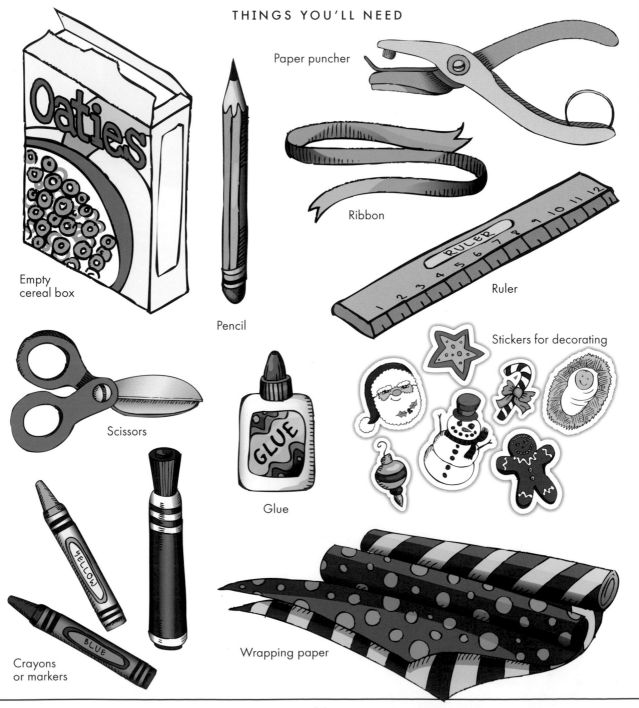

Empty
cereal box

Pencil

Paper puncher

Ribbon

Ruler

Stickers for decorating

Scissors

Glue

Crayons
or markers

Wrapping paper

DIRECTIONS

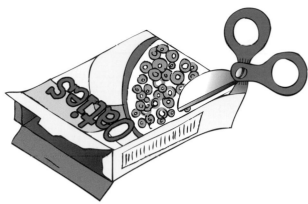

1 Cut out the front of the cereal box.

2 With your ruler and pencil, divide the box front into strips. Each strip should be 1 inch wide by 6 inches long.

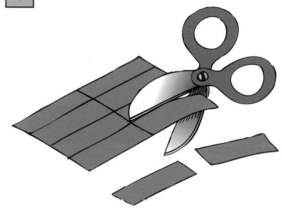

3 Cut the strips apart with your scissors.

4 Decorate the strips with your markers, crayons, wrapping paper, and stickers.

5 Use the hole puncher to make a hole in the top of each bookmark. Tie a piece of your ribbon through the hole.

Napkin Rings

Napkin rings make special gifts for parents, grandparents, and teachers.

THINGS YOU'LL NEED

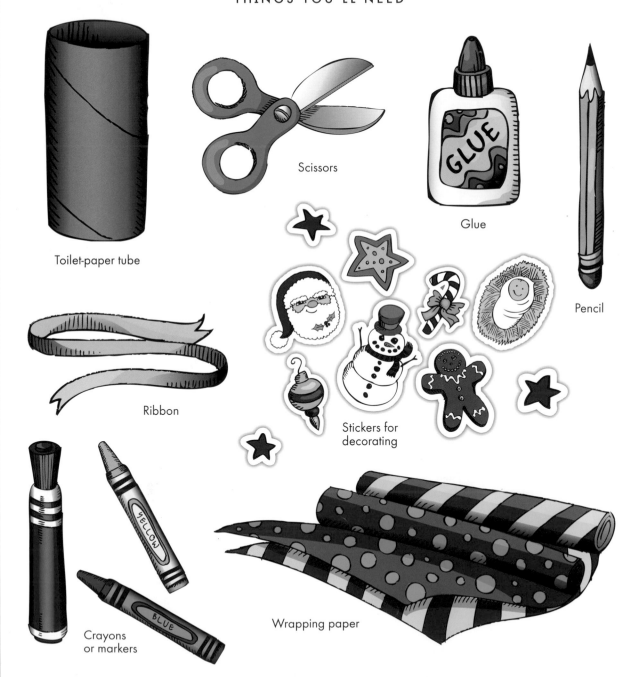

Toilet-paper tube

Scissors

Glue

Pencil

Ribbon

Stickers for decorating

Crayons or markers

Wrapping paper

DIRECTIONS

1 Lay the toilet-paper tube flat. Use your scissors to cut it in half.

2 Draw on the strips of wrapping paper with markers and crayons.

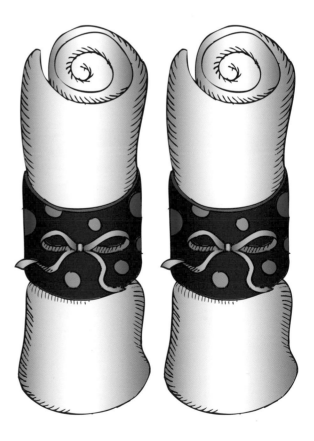

3 Decorate the tube by gluing on your wrapping paper and stickers.

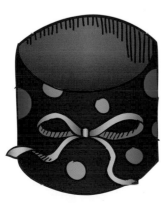

4 Glue a ribbon on the tube.

5 Carefully pull a napkin through the holder. You should be able to make two napkin holders with one toilet-paper tube.

Christmas Cards

Giving cards is a very popular idea. You can send them
to friends, teachers, and other special people.

THINGS YOU'LL NEED

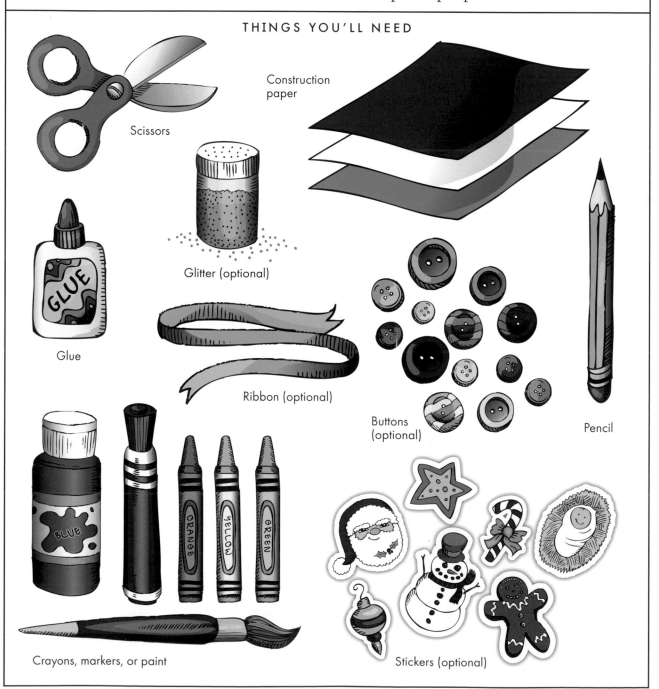

Scissors

Construction
paper

Glue

Glitter (optional)

Ribbon (optional)

Buttons
(optional)

Pencil

BLUE

ORANGE YELLOW GREEN

Crayons, markers, or paint

Stickers (optional)

DIRECTIONS FOR CARD ONE

1 Fold the paper to the size you want your card to be. Folding it once will make a large card. Folding it twice will make a small card.

2 Decorate the front of the card using paint, markers, crayons, or stickers. Write a message on the inside of the card. Don't forget to sign your name.

DIRECTIONS FOR CARD TWO

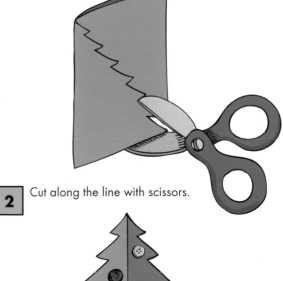

1 Draw a **jagged** line as shown from the top left corner to the bottom right corner.

2 Cut along the line with scissors.

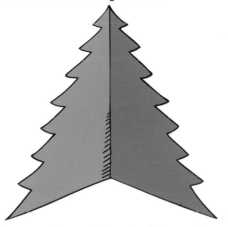

3 Now open the card. You should see a Christmas-tree shape.

4 Decorate the Christmas-tree card. Buttons make great ornaments. Write a message on the inside and sign your card.

Envelopes

You can make your own envelopes to fit your homemade cards.

THINGS YOU'LL NEED

Scissors

Pencil

Construction paper, wrapping paper, or a paper bag.

Tape or glue

GLUE

Ruler

DIRECTIONS TO MAKE A SQUARE ENVELOPE

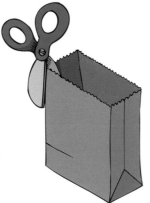
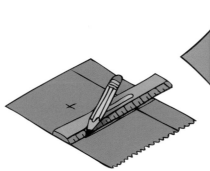

1 Cut out the front of a plain paper bag.

2 Use your ruler and pencil to mark a square that is 8 inches long on each side. This will be big enough for a 5 ¼-inch card. Mark an "x" in the center of your square (4 inches in from each side).

3 Fold three of the corners so they cover the "x." Tape or glue the corners so they'll stay in place.

4 Place your card inside. Fold the top down and tape it shut.

DIRECTIONS TO MAKE AN ENVELOPE THAT'S NOT SQUARE

1 Use your ruler and pencil to mark a square on a large piece of construction paper or wrapping paper. The paper must be 4 inches taller and 5 inches wider than your card. Draw a line 2 inches down from the top.

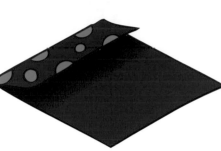

2 Fold the top down along the line.

3 Place your card under this flap.

4 Fold in each side over your card.

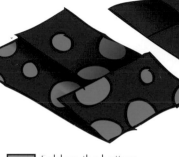

5 Fold up the bottom.

6 Now take your card out of the envelope.

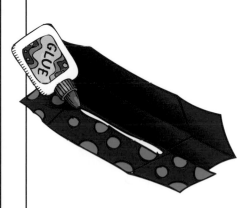

7 Glue the sides of your envelope together. Don't glue the top, however! You have to be able to put your card back inside!

8 Fold up the bottom and glue it in place.

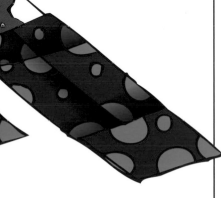

9 Put your card back inside. Fold down the top flap and tape the envelope shut.

Activities

Christmas is one of the best times to share with family and friends. Here are some fun things to do together.

1 Have a card-making party. Tell everyone to bring something different for decorating the cards. Then follow the directions on pages 18 and 19 to make lots of cards!

2 Decorate your house or your classroom together. Have everyone choose a craft from this book. Then make the crafts while you listen to Christmas music. When everyone is finished, decorate the whole house or classroom.

3 Play a dress-up game. Fill a bag full of things to wear. Make sure there are some silly hats and funny glasses! Play some Christmas music, and have everyone sit in a circle. While the music is playing, pass the bag around. When the music stops, the person holding the bag must shut their eyes and take something out of the bag. They must wear it for the rest of the game. Keep playing until all the items in the bag are gone!

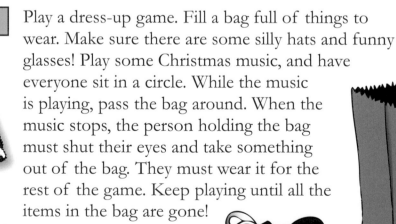

Glossary

anlters (ANT-lurz) Antlers are the bony structures that grow from the heads of deer, reindeer, moose, and elk.

christians (KRISS-chunz) Christians are people who believe that a man named Jesus was the Son of God. Christians believe Christmas is Jesus's birthday.

cultures (KUL-churz) Cultures are people's ways of life and traditions. Christmas is celebrated in many cultures.

directions (dir-EK-shunz) Directions are the steps for how to do something. You should follow the directions in this book to make your crafts.

divide (div-EYD) To divide something is to split it into parts.

holiday (HOL-uh-day) A holiday is a time for celebration, such as Easter or Valentine's Day. Christmas is a holiday.

jagged (JAG-ged) A jagged line is one that makes a zigzag.

Find More Crafts

BOOKS

Press, Judy, and Sarah Rakitin Cole (illustrator). *Big Fun Christmas Crafts & Activities*. Nashville, TN: Williamson Books, 2006.

Ross, Kathy, and Sharon Lane Holm (illustrator). *Best Christmas Crafts Ever!* Brookfield, CT: Millbrook Press, 2002.

WEB SITES

Visit our Web site for links to more crafts: childsworld.com/links

Note to Parents, Teachers, and Librarians: We routinely verify our Web links to make sure they are safe and active sites. So encourage your readers to check them out!

Index

ABOUT THE AUTHOR

Jean Eick has written over 200 books for children over the past forty years. She has written biographies, craft books, and many titles on nature and science. Jean lives in Lake Tahoe with her husband and enjoys hiking in the mountains, reading, and doing volunteer work.